To those who stood for clarity when it would've been easier to stay silent—
the strangers, the outcasts, the torchbearers.
And to those yet to stand—
may this book find you before the fog does.
To my son Elias Houssine, and all children of this ummah—
May you inherit a creed that is clear, fierce, and untamed.
Not frozen in books. Not filtered for comfort.
But burning with the same fire that moved mountains.
To the one quietly holding the line—
In the classroom, the boardroom, the masjid, or the group chat.
You're not alone.
And you're not wrong for standing.

"When the desert Bedouin heard 'La ilaha illa Allah,' he didn't ask for footnotes—he surrendered."
"Indeed, We have made this (Qur'an) easy to remember. So is there any who will remember?"
—Surah al-Qamar (54:17)
"They asked for clarity. You were sent to carry it."
"When the world calls confusion mercy and doubt humility, clarity becomes rebellion."
"A people once moved by a single sentence now drown in endless opinions."

— ABDELLATIF RAJI

CONTENTS

FOREWORD

There is a difference between religion and creed.

Religion can be inherited, memorized, performed on autopilot.

But **creed** — real, rooted īmān — must be *chosen*. It must be *defended*. It must be *clear*.

We live in a time where Muslims have more access to knowledge than ever before — and yet more confusion, more doubt, and more fragility in belief.

This is not a lack of content.

This is a crisis of clarity.

The Flame of Clarity is not just another book about aqīdah.

It is a declaration of war on everything that has blurred the truth.

The author writes not as a theologian from above, but as a brother from within — someone who has felt the fog, fought through it, and now offers us a map out.

Each chapter is a confrontation:

- With the lies we've absorbed
- With the fears we've normalized
- With the silence we've justified

But more importantly, each chapter is a call back:

To **simplicity without ignorance,**

To **strength without arrogance**,

To **submission without shame**.

This book reminds us that clarity is not a luxury — it's a lifeline. And those who carry it into the next generation are not just teachers.

They are **torchbearers**.

To the reader:

Don't skim this book. Sit with it. Let it burn.

Because what you hold in your hands is not just theology. It's a **battle manual** for the age of ideological war.

And if you let it reach your heart, you will not walk away the same.

— A fellow student of clarity

PREFACE

"They told us to just believe. They never taught us how to stand."

I did not write this book to add to your bookshelf.

I wrote it because I saw something breaking — quietly, slowly, and all around me.

I saw Muslims who still said *La ilaha illa Allah*

—but no longer knew what it meant.

I saw youth raised in practicing homes

—but unable to explain why they believed anything at all.

I saw people who loved Islam

—but were too intellectually paralyzed to defend it when it mattered.

I saw scholars debating in clouds

—while the ummah collapsed on the ground.

And I realized:

We are not suffering from a lack of access.

We are drowning in information.

What we're missing is **conviction.**

Clarity.

Creed that cuts through the fog and dares to say: *This is the truth.*

Islam Was Never Meant To Be This Complicated

The first generations believed with simplicity, not shallowness.

They didn't need 14-volume explanations of tawḥīd.

They heard a sentence—and they surrendered.

Today, we ask for nuance before obedience.

We delay certainty until it's popular.

We hide truth under a blanket of academic politeness.

And we wonder why our children leave Islam feeling confused, unsure, and exhausted.

This book is a refusal to let that continue.

This Is A Call To Ideological Awakening

Not just spiritual revival.

Not just personal reform.

But a full return to **creed as clarity**, as **resistance**, and as **the foundation of everything**.

What you believe about Allah, His Book, His decree, and His sovereignty is not a private opinion.

It is a lens through which you see the world.

It is the compass that steers your family, your politics, your desires, your fears, your identity, and your children's futures.

When that compass is cracked — everything collapses.

This Book Is A Weapon, Not A Pillow

It is not gentle with confusion.

It does not flatter doubt.

It will not praise "intellectual humility" when it is really just spiritual surrender.

This book is for those who are tired of fog.

Tired of inherited Islam that feels fragile.

Tired of TikTok theologians, soft sermons, and apologetic khutbahs that say nothing clearly.

This book is for the ones who want to build — and rebuild — a **creed that can survive the storm**.

My Hope For You

My hope is that you finish this book with:

- A heart on fire
- A mind unshaken
- A creed you can explain with clarity and defend with courage
- And a deep resolve to pass it on — to your children, your students, your friends — not as tradition, but as *truth*

This is not just about aqīdah.

It's about **survival**.

It's about **legacy**.

It's about **becoming the generation that brought the fire back.**

Let's begin.

La ilaha illa Allah.

Not just spoken.

Lived.

ACKNOWLEDGMENTS

To the critics, the questioners, and the doubters who forced me to sharpen my clarity and deepen my submission — you are more part of this book than you know.

To the **friends and companions** who read drafts, pushed deadlines, prayed during delays, or reminded me to keep going when the fog crept in again — this is our book, not just mine.

To my **family**, who bore the weight of this mission — in silence, in patience, and in sacrifice — may Allah protect you and make this creed your comfort as it became mine.

And to the reader:

You are the one I wrote this for.

If this book found you in confusion, I pray it leaves you in conviction.

If it struck a match, don't let the fire die.

Pass it on.

PROLOGUE

"One sentence once moved the world. Now we barely feel it move us."

There was a time when one sentence made tyrants tremble.

It had no footnotes.

No theology degree attached.

No translator needed.

It was clear. Absolute.

And when it was spoken, it split the world in two:

La ilaha illa Allah.

There is no deity worthy of worship but Allah.

It was not a phrase. It was a **revolution**.

A line in the sand.

A sword drawn against falsehood.

A fire that burned away idols — not just the ones made of stone, but the ones made of pride, tribe, ego, empire.

This one sentence built a civilization.

Empires fell before it.

Lives were lost for it.

Hearts surrendered to it in seconds.

Now?

We wear it on chains.

Recite it by habit.

Scroll past it.

And when it is questioned, many of us cannot explain it — or worse, cannot defend it.

We know how to say it.

But do we know how to **live it**?

That question is why this book exists.

Because the flame hasn't gone out.

It's just been buried under layers of fog, fear, philosophy, and forgetfulness.

This book is here to **dig it up, clean it off, and set it ablaze again.**

So if you've ever felt the fog pressing in —

If you've ever wondered why belief feels harder now than ever —

If you've ever feared that your children might not hold onto this dīn —

If you've ever whispered *La ilaha illa Allah* and wished it felt more alive in your bones —

Then read on.

The clarity is still there.

The fire still burns.

You don't need a new creed.

You need to return to the original.

And light it.

INTRODUCTION

"This book is not a lecture. It's a lit match."

Why This Book Exists

You're not holding a typical book on Islamic theology.

You won't find lengthy footnotes here.

You won't find debates over abstract theological terms.

You won't find neutrality, softness, or compromise.

Instead, you'll find something else:

Fire. Urgency. Simplicity. Resistance. Clarity.

Because this isn't just a book.

It's a **call to ideological awakening** in a time of deep spiritual sleep.

Most Muslims today are not leaving Islam out of rebellion.

They're drifting away from it out of **confusion**.

They've inherited rituals, but not reasons.

They've memorized facts, but lost meaning.

They say *La ilaha illa Allah* — but few could explain what it demands.

This book is a response to that crisis.

What This Book Will Do For You

It will not entertain you.

It will **confront you**.

You will learn:

- Why clarity in creed is not optional — it's **the foundation of survival**
- How foreign philosophies hijacked our discourse and diluted our faith
- What the Six Pillars of Īmān really mean — **not in theory, but in your life**
- How to protect your heart from modern spiritual subversion
- How to raise a new generation of believers who **stand when others fold**
- How to **live, teach, and defend creed** in a world that demands silence

How This Book Is Structured

This book is divided into **three parts**:

1. **The Cracked Mirror** – how we lost the clarity
2. **The Pure Spring** – how we rebuild from the source
3. **The Torchbearers** – how we prepare a generation to carry it forward

Each chapter ends with a **Clarity Challenge** — a practical step to live what you've learned.

This is not theory.

This is transformation.

What This Book Is Not

This is not:

- A deep dive into kalām or sectarian polemics
- A commentary on historical theological schools
- A feel-good read for someone who wants to stay in the gray

This is a book for Muslims who are **done with confusion**.

Who want to stop guessing, doubting, and explaining away.

Who are ready to say:

"I believe. I submit. I stand."

Why You Should Keep Reading

Because this isn't just about belief.

It's about **how you live.**

How you **raise your children.**

How you **teach your students.**

How you **worship under pressure.**

How you **answer when truth is mocked.**

And how you **hold the line when everyone else folds.**

This book will not just inform you.

It will **form you.**

Not into a scholar.

But into a **torchbearer**.

One who walks into the storm holding the **flame of clarity** high—
for everyone behind them to see.

Now turn the page.

The fog is lifting.

The fire is coming back.

PART I: THE CRACKED MIRROR

How We Lost the Clarity

Once, belief was simple. Strong. Clear.

When the Prophet ﷺ spoke, hearts surrendered. When the Qur'an was recited, lives changed. *La ilaha illa Allah* wasn't a slogan — it was a sword that split falsehood from truth.

But now? We inherit belief like a family heirloom: intact in language, cracked in meaning. We repeat the words without realizing we're staring into a broken mirror — fragments of a creed we never fully absorbed.

In this section, we confront the uncomfortable truth:

We didn't lose Islam. We lost the clarity that made Islam live.

You'll walk through:

The rise of cultural Islam and the fall of conviction

How foreign ideologies invaded the masjid disguised as scholarship

The battle our ancestors fought to protect creed — and why we've forgotten it

How complexity became a cover for confusion — and why clarity was always the Prophet's ﷺ way

This is where the journey begins. Not with answers — but with honesty.

Before we rebuild the flame, we must face the fog.

CHAPTER 1: A GENERATION IN THE FOG

"The first step toward clarity is admitting you're lost."

We Inherited Confusion

We were born into fog.

We didn't choose it. We didn't ask for it. But we live in it every day.

A fog that blurs truth until it's just an opinion. That turns certainties into slogans. That takes a creed forged in fire—**La ilaha illa Allah**—and recites it like a ritual, not a revolution.

Ask a young Muslim today, "What is your faith?"

You'll often hear words like "I believe in God," or "I'm spiritual," or "I try my best."

What you won't hear is conviction.

What you rarely hear is clarity.

We are a generation raised on diluted slogans, not prophetic sentences. Our faith is often **secondhand, ceremonial, and soft**—not lived, not loved, and certainly not fought for.

Cultural Islam Vs. Creedal Islam

Somewhere along the way, Islam became **a culture before it remained a creed**.

We fast in Ramadan but forget why we restrain desire.

We pray but don't pause to ask *who we are standing before*.

We say "Inshallah" like a social reflex—not a declaration of divine will.

We attend Jum'ah but sleep through the soul of the khutbah.

Islam became performance.

Creed became decoration.

And the results are devastating.

We produce youth who can navigate apps but not doubts. Who memorize the surahs but can't explain *why* they believe. Who defend identity, but not **ideology**.

When Islam is inherited, not internalized, **doubt becomes destiny**.

Information, But No Illumination

We are drowning in content, but starving for clarity.

YouTube is full of lectures. TikTok has a thousand muftis. Instagram feeds us filtered fiqh.

But something is still missing.

Our problem is not a lack of access. It's a lack of **anchor**.

The Salaf didn't need terabytes of theology to believe. They needed one sentence.

La ilaha illa Allah.

No deity worthy of worship but Allah.

That sentence created an empire. Today, it barely sustains an Instagram caption.

How did we lose its fire?

Faith Is Now Fragile

We have built our faith on sand. Not the Qur'an, not Sunnah—but on emotion, tribalism, culture, and identity politics.

So when life hits—when the university professor mocks you, when social media floods you with doubts, when the world calls your values "extreme"—**you crumble**.

Because what you thought was faith was just inherited fog.

This chapter is not here to blame you.

It's here to wake you.

What Clarity Demands

Clarity begins with courage—the courage to say:

"I don't fully understand what I believe."

"I've been repeating words I've never fully felt."

"I want creed that cuts through confusion, not adds to it."

This book will not give you opinions.

It will not entertain you with nuance.

It will take you back to the **source**. Back to the **fire**. Back to the **sentence that split nations and united hearts**.

La ilaha illa Allah.

Clarity Challenge: Before You Turn The Page

Find a quiet place. Sit for five minutes.

Ask yourself this, out loud:

"What do I *actually* mean when I say 'La ilaha illa Allah'?"

"If someone asked me to explain it—not academically, but from the heart—what would I say?"

Write your answer down.

Not a Google answer. **Your answer**.

That is where we begin.

CHAPTER 2: WHEN FOREIGN GODS ENTERED THE MOSQUE

"They didn't break the creed. They diluted it—drop by drop, word by word."

The Mosque Was Once A Fortress

There was a time when the mosque was not just a place of prayer.

It was a fortress of truth. A bastion of tawḥīd.

You didn't walk into it carrying your own ideas—you walked in to surrender them.

But that fortress was breached. Not by swords. Not by armies.

But by language, by ideas, by alien gods wearing scholarly robes.

The Philosophers Knocked… And We Let Them In

The early Muslims had something the world couldn't understand: a creed so pure, it didn't require embellishment.

God said it. They believed it. They lived it.

But then came the Greeks.

Plato. Aristotle. Neoplatonism. Logic. Metaphysics. Abstract causes. The One and the Many.

To the untrained mind, these sounded "deep." To the insecure Muslim intellect, they sounded "necessary."

So we began importing.

We told ourselves:

"Islam can benefit from this."

"Aql (reason) must have its rightful place."

"We must refute them using their tools."

But here's the danger: **When you borrow a god's tools, you borrow his assumptions.**

And just like that, foreign frameworks began to shape how we defined our Lord.

From Revelation To Rationalization

Suddenly, tawḥīd wasn't just believed—it had to be **philosophically proven**.

God's attributes weren't accepted—they were **debated, parsed, redefined**.

The Qur'an wasn't enough—**"first principles"** and Greek logic now had to validate it.

And so the creed once learned in minutes became buried under jargon:

- Essence vs. attributes
- Contingency vs. necessity
- Temporal origination
- Modalities of speech

The Bedouin surrendered with a sentence. The theologian took thirty years.

What We Lost

In trying to sound intelligent, we forgot how to sound sincere.

We built castles of logic, but they couldn't hold faith.

We defined Allah in defense, but forgot how to **submit**.

We debated His names while ignoring His **commands**.

And most dangerously: we began to **fear looking simplistic** more than we feared **misrepresenting the divine**.

Creed Became An Experiment

With foreign ideas came **foreign priorities**:

- Certainty was replaced with speculation
- Revelation became secondary to reason
- The words of the Prophet ﷺ were treated as *maybe*
- The consensus of the Sahabah became *optional*

And then came the sects. Each carving out their brand of Islam. Each redefining Allah through their lens.

Each claiming to defend truth—while dragging the ummah into confusion.

And the people?

They were left watching scholars fight in the clouds while their own faith crumbled on the ground.

The Salaf Fought Back

But not all stayed silent.

Imām Aḥmad stood like a mountain during the Mihnah.

He was offered the world if he'd just bend his words about the

Qur'an.

He refused. He suffered. He was lashed. But he protected the creed.

Imām Mālik famously said:

"Istiwā' is known, how is unknown, belief in it is obligatory, and questioning it is an innovation."

No long lectures. No footnotes.

Just clarity. Just surrender.

These men were not anti-intellectual. They were anti-infiltration.

Clarity Means Knowing Where To Draw The Line

This chapter isn't calling you to abandon thought.

It's calling you to **anchor it**.

Use your mind—but don't let it become your god.

Study logic—but never let it replace the **light of revelation**.

Debate if you must—but only after you've *believed* like the first generation did: immediately, completely, and without arrogance.

Clarity Challenge: Intellectual Detox

For one day, unplug from podcasts, YouTube debates, and social media takes.

Sit with the Qur'an. Read it not to *analyze*, but to **surrender**.

Then ask yourself:

"Have I made understanding God more complicated than obeying Him?"

If so, it's time to return to the **source**.

To remove the fog of philosophy.

To rebuild a creed that doesn't *sound* profound—it **is**.

CHAPTER 3: THE BATTLE FOR THE SOUL OF 'AQĪDAH

"They preserved it with blood. We abandon it with silence."

Creed Has Always Been A Battlefield

Don't let the modern calm fool you.

What you believe today—your ability to say "Allah is above His throne," or "The Qur'an is uncreated," or "Faith increases and decreases"—wasn't always safe to say.

At one point in our history, those sentences could get you **whipped, imprisoned, or executed**.

Yes, today you can scroll past theology. But once, men were **tortured for it**.

Because **'Aqīdah isn't a side issue. It's the soul of Islam.**

The Mihnah: When Belief Was Put On Trial

It began with an idea—one imported, dressed in reason:

"The Qur'an is created."

At first, it seemed academic. A harmless phrase. A fine point of theology.

But behind it lurked a monster: **if the Qur'an is created, it can be dismissed, edited, subordinated.**

This was no small claim. It struck at the root of revelation. If the Qur'an is created, then it is **not divine in essence**—it is a product, not a Word.

The Abbasid rulers backed the claim. **State-sponsored theology.** Scholars were summoned and forced to agree—or suffer.

Some complied.

Some gave vague answers.

But one man stood.

Imām Aḥmad: One Man Against An Empire

He was no warrior. He held no office.

But Imām Aḥmad ibn Ḥanbal became the shield of the ummah when the creed was under attack.

He was arrested, beaten, publicly humiliated.

They said: *"Say the Qur'an is created."*

He said: *"Bring me something clearer than the Qur'an and Sunnah, and I will follow it."*

They said: *"All the scholars agree."*

He said: *"The truth is not known by men—it is known by evidence."*

He didn't write a long refutation.

He stood—and that was enough.

The Fire That Purified The Creed

This was no petty intellectual quarrel. This was a war over *what kind of Islam would survive.*

- An Islam built on **revelation** or **rational reinterpretation**?
- A faith where Allah is described **as He describes Himself**—or one where He must first pass philosophical approval?
- A creed of **clarity and submission**, or of **doubt and debate**?

Through Aḥmad's trial, the message echoed:

"Creed is not negotiable. The soul of Islam is not for sale."

And when the people saw him stand, the tide began to turn. Eventually, the rulers reversed course. The storm passed. But the scars remained.

And the line in the sand was drawn for all time.

The Real Meaning Of Salafīyah

Some hear the word "Salafī" and think of narrow minds or cultural conservatism.

But Salafīyah—true Salafīyah—is not a sect. It is the **preservation of clarity**.

It is loyalty to the way the Prophet ﷺ and his companions believed —not just what they believed.

- They didn't redefine tawḥīd—they **lived it**.
- They didn't debate the meaning of "istiwa"—they **affirmed it and moved on**.
- They didn't wait for a council to decide what to believe—they had the Qur'an, the Sunnah, and **no doubt**.

This is not nostalgia. It's the original blueprint.

Why This Battle Still Rages

Today, the language is softer. The lashes are gone.

But the battle for 'Aqīdah is not over. It has just gone digital.

Instead of inquisitions, we have **influencers**.

Instead of philosophical terms, we have **postmodern doubt**.

Instead of rulers enforcing theology, we have **social media mob logic** redefining "good" Islam.

But the stakes are the same:

Will you **surrender to what Allah said about Himself**—or to what sounds more fashionable in a TED Talk?

Choose Your Side

This is not a call to sectarianism.

It is a call to **loyalty**.

To the Ummah of Clarity. The Ummah that stood when it was hard to stand.

The Ummah that believed before it understood, because they trusted the One who spoke.

"We hear and we obey."

That was their slogan.

Let it be yours.

Clarity Challenge: Loyalty Check

Tonight, ask yourself in prayer:

"If Allah described Himself in a way that offends modern minds, would I submit—or reinterpret?"

"Am I shaping my faith around revelation—or around comfort?"

Then open the Qur'an. Read the verses about Allah's names and attributes.

Don't explain them away. Don't philosophize.

Affirm. Believe. Stand.

Like Aḥmad did.

CHAPTER 4: COMPLEXITY KILLS CONVICTION

"Clarity doesn't come from knowing more. It comes from knowing what matters."

We Are Addicted To Complication

The modern Muslim is overfed and undernourished.

We chase answers to questions no Companion ever asked.

We memorize charts of theological nuance but still doubt Allah's plan.

We can explain the cosmological argument, but can't pray without distraction.

We scroll through one-hour debates on divine attributes—then miss Fajr.

Somewhere along the way, we started believing a **deadly lie**:

"The more complex my faith sounds, the deeper it must be."

But here's the truth:

Conviction thrives in simplicity. Confusion hides in complication.

Belief Was Never Meant To Be A Puzzle

When the Prophet ﷺ said "La ilaha illa Allah," people didn't reply:

"Could you define 'ilah' according to a Greek metaphysical framework?"

They **believed.**

Immediately. Completely. Viscerally.

When Jibrīl came to teach the faith, he didn't deliver a philosophy lecture.

He asked five questions.

The Prophet ﷺ answered.

"You have spoken the truth." Done.

No citations. No commentaries. No ten-part video series.

Islam was clear. Because Allah made it clear.

"And We did not send down to you the Book except that you may make clear to them that over which they differed."

—Surah an-Naḥl (16:64)

Complexity Builds Walls, Not Doors

The early generations opened doors. Today's discourse builds walls:

- Walls of jargon.
- Walls of intellectual elitism.
- Walls that say, *"You can't understand Islam unless you've read 14 books on ontology."*

This is not scholarship. This is **gatekeeping disguised as depth.**

And for the average Muslim? It creates **spiritual paralysis**.

They feel too small to believe, too ignorant to be confident.

They think faith is a mountain they'll never climb—when in truth, it was meant to meet them where they stand.

When Overthinking Becomes A Trap

A man once came to Imām Mālik asking about a verse:

"The Most Merciful rose above the Throne…" (Qur'an 20:5)

He said, "How did He rise?"

Mālik's face changed.

"The rising is known. The how is unknown. Belief in it is obligatory. Asking about it is innovation."

That's not anti-intellectualism.

That's **intellectual humility**.

Not every question needs an answer.

And not every answer strengthens faith.

Some answers **feed the ego**. Others **feed the soul**.

Why The Prophet Didn't Teach A Curriculum

Have you ever wondered why the Prophet ﷺ didn't leave behind theological textbooks?

Why he didn't teach "Islam 101" in structured courses?

Because he was building **believers**, not academics.

Conviction, not complexity.

Action, not abstraction.

The Sahabah didn't learn faith the way we do today.

They lived with the Prophet.

They saw how he walked, spoke, cried, forgave.

Every moment was creed in motion.

That's why when they heard, *"Believe in Allah,"* they **didn't ask for definitions**.

They **submitted**.

The Enemy: Academic Pride

Let's be honest.

Sometimes we chase complex explanations not to get closer to Allah—but to impress others.

We quote scholars to win debates. We read difficult books to sound profound.

We mistake sounding smart for being guided.

And in doing so, we lose the childlike faith that made the early Muslims invincible.

"Whoever humbles himself for Allah, He will raise him."

—Prophet Muhammad ﷺ

You don't need a PhD to know your Lord.

You need a clean heart and a willing soul.

What Clarity Looks Like

Here's what clarity feels like:

- You can explain your faith in one breath.
- You can teach it to a child.
- You can live it under pressure.
- You don't panic when asked, "Why do you believe?"

Clarity doesn't reject depth—it **orders** it.

You start from the ground, not the clouds.

"Say: Allah is One."

That's where it starts. That's where it *always* starts.

Clarity Challenge: The 60-Second Test

Try this:

Imagine someone stops you on the street and says,

"What do you believe as a Muslim? But explain it to me like I'm 10 years old."

Write your answer in **60 seconds or less**. No jargon. No footnotes.

Just you, your Lord, and the truth.

Can you do it?

Because that's not just a challenge. That's **the foundation** of conviction.

PART II: THE PURE SPRING

Rebuilding Creed from the Source

Clarity was never lost because the source ran dry.

It was lost because we stopped drawing from it.

The Qur'an is still clear.

The Prophet's ﷺ method still works.

The early generations still show the way.

This section is about **returning** — not to nostalgia, but to **original strength**.

Here, you'll rediscover the **Six Pillars of Īmān** as more than doctrines — they're **daily engines** that reshape how you think, act, worship, and lead.

You'll walk through:

The raw simplicity and power of the core beliefs — and how they transform your life

How the Companions absorbed īmān **without delay, hesitation, or debate**

What it really means to live under divine sovereignty — not just as a belief, but as law

How to **preach creed like fire, not ice** — so it spreads, inspires, and takes root

This part isn't about learning new information.

It's about **realigning your life with eternal truths**.

You're not just rebuilding creed —

You're **drinking from the pure spring again.**

CHAPTER 5: THE UNSHAKEABLE SIX – HOW THE PILLARS POWER A LIVED FAITH

"Belief isn't what you say—it's what you build your life on."

From Fog To Foundation

We've spent four chapters cutting through confusion. Now we return to the ground beneath our feet.

Six beliefs.

That's it.

Not sixty. Not six hundred. Six.

They are not categories in a textbook. They are **the architecture of reality**.

And when lived—not just memorized—they make you unshakable.

This is not about "having faith." This is about living like the world was built on it.

Why Allah Began With The Basics

When Jibrīl came to the Prophet ﷺ in the famous hadith, he asked:

"What is Īmān?"

The Prophet ﷺ replied:

"To believe in Allah, His angels, His books, His messengers, the Last Day, and in the divine decree, both good and bad."

He didn't start with aqīdah terminologies.

He didn't say, "Learn the schools of theology first."

He gave us six truths. That's it.

Why?

Because **simplicity is not weakness—it's power.**

These six are the load-bearing beams of the soul.

When they're strong, life makes sense. Pain has purpose. Worship feels weighty.

When they're missing, everything collapses—slowly, silently, then all at once.

Let's revive them.

1. Belief In Allah: The Anchor Of All Meaning

Belief in Allah isn't just that He exists.

It's that He **owns you**, **knows you**, and **guides you**.

When you live this, stress shrinks. Doubts dissolve. Ego dies.

It's no longer "What do *I* want from life?"

It becomes: *"What does Allah want from me today?"*

Belief in Allah transforms anxiety into submission, confusion into direction, and hardship into purification.

It's not philosophy. It's surrender.

2. Belief In The Angels: The Unseen Witnesses

You are never alone.

The moment you believe in angels—not abstractly, but *existentially*—everything changes.

- You guard your tongue because two scribes are writing.
- You walk with dignity because the noble angels are watching.
- You make decisions knowing that **Gabriel once descended for men who feared Allah in secret**.

Belief in angels builds **accountability**, **presence**, and **awe**.

3. Belief In The Books: Light In A Dark World

These books aren't ancient scriptures. They are living guidance.

You believe in the Torah, the Gospel, and especially the Qur'an—not as history, but as **legislation and lifeblood**.

Belief in books means:

- You don't guess what's right—you open the Book.
- You don't follow your feelings—you follow revelation.
- You don't trust trends—you trust truth.

The Qur'an isn't just read. It's *followed*.

When you believe it, you let it **interrupt you**, **reshape you**, and **save you**.

4. Belief In The Messengers: Loyalty To The Legacy

To believe in the messengers is to love **truth over trend**.

You don't just admire them—you **follow them**, **obey them**, **defend them**.

It's not enough to know Muhammad ﷺ is the last Prophet.

You must see him as your **role model, your commander, and your compass**.

Belief in messengers is what keeps you from reinventing religion.

It keeps you loyal to the path when modernity begs you to rewrite it.

5. Belief In The Last Day: Urgency And Direction

This is the **ultimate recalibration**.

If you truly believe the Day of Judgment is coming:

- You don't scroll mindlessly.
- You don't sleep through salah.
- You don't chase approval from those who can't save you from Hell.

The Last Day isn't a theory. It's a **deadline**.

And if you knew your deadline, you would live with urgency, repentance, and purpose.

Belief in the Hereafter turns distraction into devotion.

6. Belief In Divine Decree: Peace With The Plan

Here's where most people collapse.

They believe in God, prayer, the Qur'an—but when things go wrong, they break.

Why? Because they never internalized:

"What hit you was never meant to miss. What missed you was never meant to hit."

Belief in qadar isn't fatalism. It's freedom.

It frees you from regret, resentment, and control-freak anxiety.

It teaches you to act **with full trust**, to try **without panic**, and to grieve **without despair**.

This is the backbone of tawakkul. Without it, even Muslims live in emotional ruin.

The Six Pillars Are A System, Not Just Statements

Each of these beliefs affects:

- How you think
- How you act
- How you interpret everything that happens to you

Together, they form a **complete worldview**: a way of seeing the world with divine perspective.

Without them, you're living blind—even if you're religious.

What Happens When You Don't Believe These Fully

- You'll trust horoscopes more than qadar.
- You'll love influencers more than messengers.
- You'll look for healing in podcasts and forget the Qur'an.
- You'll fear cameras more than angels.
- You'll believe in God, but live like He's uninvolved.
- You'll live like this world is final—because you forgot the next one.

That's not just weak īmān.

That's a **shattered operating system**.

Clarity Challenge: Make The Pillars Move

For the next 6 days, take one pillar a day.

Ask yourself, honestly:

"If I truly believed this, what would change in how I live?"

Then make one small change for each.

Write it down. Live it out.

When the Six Pillars go from memory to movement—**clarity is born.**

CHAPTER 6: WHAT THE COMPANIONS KNEW THAT WE FORGOT

"They didn't ask for definitions. They asked, 'What should I do?'"

The Difference Was Immediate

We often assume the Prophet ﷺ had years to train his companions. He didn't.

Some only met him once. Others for days. Some never saw him again after a single encounter.

But those brief moments *moved mountains*.

- A man would hear *La ilaha illa Allah* and **change the direction of his entire life**.
- A woman would embrace Islam and **risk everything** to preserve it.
- A slave would whisper "Ahad, Ahad" as whips tore his flesh —because he'd tasted **conviction**.

How?

Because their hearts weren't asking, *"Is this intellectually satisfying?"*

They were asking, *"Is this true—and what does it demand of me?"*

They Believed With Their Hearts—Not Just Their Heads

Today, we treat faith like a slow download.

We need reassurance, content, cross-referencing, YouTube playlists, long debates.

The Companions didn't wait to believe.

"The moment belief entered their hearts, their lives followed."

When the verses came down, they didn't say,

"Let me do some research and get back to you."

They said,

"We hear and we obey."

Their īmān wasn't fragile.

Because it wasn't built on approval—it was built on surrender.

When Belief Cost Something, They Paid It

Bilāl could have stayed quiet.

Sumayyah could have played along.

Khabbāb could have fled.

But they didn't.

Why?

Because they knew faith wasn't a *label*—it was a **loyalty**.

A Companion would be **tortured, exiled, insulted, killed**—but you couldn't pull īmān from his chest.

Today, we fold under an Instagram comment.

We second-guess our religion when someone raises a doubt.

We delay submission until we've read three books and two threads.

They said "yes" to Allah with scars.

We say "maybe" with comfort.

They Didn't Separate Learning From Living

Some of us want to "learn Islam" before we live it.

The Companions didn't wait.

They **prayed while learning**.

They **obeyed before understanding**.

They **acted with what they knew**, and trusted Allah for the rest.

When a verse came down, they didn't say,

"I'll reflect on this deeply."

They **changed behavior that same day**.

That's īmān in motion.

They Had Faith That Translated Into Habits

Faith wasn't abstract for them.

- **Belief in the Last Day** meant waking for Tahajjud.
- **Belief in angels** meant controlling their tongue.
- **Belief in the Qur'an** meant they wept when it was recited.
- **Belief in qadar** meant they didn't whine when things went wrong.
- **Belief in Allah** meant they fought temptations with grit.

They didn't just believe—they **embodied**.

Their beliefs showed up in **how they slept, walked, spent, fought, and forgave**.

They Were Lit From Within

There was a spark behind their eyes.

A **certainty** you couldn't teach in a class.

Umar ibn al-Khaṭṭāb wasn't a scholar when he accepted Islam.

But the moment he did, he walked to the Kaʻbah and **declared it out loud**.

No shame. No delay.

He didn't just submit. He **led**.

This was the secret of the Sahabah:

They weren't perfect, but they were **clear**.

They didn't have all the answers—but they knew the truth when they saw it.

And they acted like it.

What We Forgot

We forgot how to believe like that.

We turned faith into theory.

We trained Muslims to **debate** before they ever **obey**.

We taught them that doubts are academic problems—when they're often spiritual ones.

We forgot that:

- **Submission heals doubt.**
- **Obedience opens clarity.**
- **Action protects the soul.**

They lived it. We dissect it.

Clarity Challenge: Believe Like A Companion

Pick one verse of the Qur'an that tells you to act.

Any verse. Even a simple one: "Establish the prayer." "Lower your gaze." "Give in charity."

Then do what the Sahabah would do:

Act on it *today*—without delay, without excuse, without needing more information.

Then ask yourself:

"What if I lived my whole life like this?"

That's how īmān catches fire again.

CHAPTER 7: DIVINE COMMAND – LIVING UNDER GOD'S SOVEREIGNTY (ḤĀKIMIYYAH)

"It's not about believing in God—it's about obeying Him when it's inconvenient."

What Is Ḥākimiyyah, Really?

Ḥākimiyyah isn't a slogan. It's not a fringe idea.

It's the **core of tawḥīd in action**.

To believe in Ḥākimiyyah is to say:

"Allah alone has the right to legislate. To define truth. To decide right and wrong."

Not the state.

Not society.

Not your feelings.

Only Him.

It's not just a theological concept. It's a **question of sovereignty**: *Who rules your life?*

The Qur'an Doesn't Whisper About It

"The command is for none but Allah."

—Surah Yūsuf (12:40)

"Is it the judgment of [Jāhiliyyah] they seek? But who is better than Allah in judgment for a people who have certainty?"

—Surah al-Mā'idah (5:50)

These aren't optional beliefs.

They are the **bedrock of la ilaha illa Allah**.

Yet today, many Muslims repeat the shahādah while quietly obeying a different lord:

- The algorithm
- The government
- Public opinion
- Self-will

Ḥākimiyyah demands we **return Allah to His rightful place: on the throne of our lives**.

This Is Bigger Than Law—It's About Loyalty

Some reduce Ḥākimiyyah to political systems.

But it starts **far more personally**.

It means:

- Allah determines what success means—not your boss.
- Allah sets moral boundaries—not popular culture.
- Allah decides family roles, business ethics, modesty, marriage—not a think tank or influencer.

If you're still asking, *"But what will people think?"*—then **they are ruling you**, not God.

Why This Principle Is So Threatening

Every prophet preached Ḥākimiyyah.

That's why every prophet was opposed by the ruling elite.

Firʿawn didn't say to Mūsā, "You can't believe in God."

He said, *"You can't disobey me."*

Nimrūd didn't say to Ibrāhīm, "You can't have your own beliefs."

He said, *"You can't challenge my authority."*

Because **the moment you say God commands all**, you expose who's been pretending to be God.

That's why this belief was and still is **revolutionary**.

We've Replaced God's Rule With Convenience

Today, many of us obey:

- Our **nafs** when it wants harām.
- The **state** when it redefines morality.
- **Society** when it mocks modesty or hijab.
- **Feminist, capitalist, secularist frameworks** that sound empowering but displace divine command.

We say, "Islam is a complete way of life"—but then treat it like a **menu**, picking what fits our preferences.

But Ḥākimiyyah isn't a suggestion. It's a **claim of ownership**.

"My prayer, my sacrifice, my life, and my death are for Allah, Lord of the worlds."

—Surah al-Anʿām (6:162)

The Prophet ﷺ Built A State On This Creed

When the Prophet migrated to Madinah, his goal wasn't just to escape persecution.

It was to **build a society under Allah's rule.**

- Laws came down.
- Justice was revealed.
- The Qur'an **governed**, not just inspired.

This was īmān with a spine.

Not personal piety only—but **public submission**.

That's why Madinah succeeded. That's why Mecca fought him.

They understood what some Muslims today have forgotten:

La ilaha illa Allah means no man has the right to override Allah.

So What Does Ḥākimiyyah Look Like Today?

No, you may not live in a fully Islamic state.

But **you can still live under God's rule**—*if you choose to.*

It starts with:

- **Legislative submission**: If Allah said it, I obey—no compromise.
- **Moral clarity**: Halal and haram are not open for debate.
- **Personal discipline**: My desires do not dictate my values.
- **Cultural resistance**: I oppose any system that opposes my Lord—gently, wisely, but firmly.
- **Public courage**: I don't hide my values at work, school, or online.

This is not extremism. It's **normal Islam, lived fully.**

What Happens When We Ignore It?

When we remove Allah's authority:

- We get **gender confusion** instead of fitrah.
- **Interest-based economies** instead of zakāh and barakah.
- **Family collapse** instead of sacred responsibility.
- **Silence on injustice** instead of speaking truth to power.
- **Selective Islam** instead of full submission.

Without Ḥākimiyyah, Islam becomes a label.

With it, Islam becomes **life.**

Clarity Challenge: Who Really Rules Your Life?

Sit alone and ask yourself:

"In my daily decisions—what to wear, who to love, what to watch, how to speak—who decides?"

"When Allah's rule clashes with my comfort, who wins?"

Now choose one area where you've been following **someone else's rules**.

Replace it—today—with divine command.

That's the beginning of Ḥākimiyyah.

Not chanting it. **Living it.**

CHAPTER 8: PREACH LIKE FIRE, NOT ICE

"You don't pass on belief by explaining it. You pass it on by burning with it."

We're Teaching Creed Like It's A Cold Lecture

We are raising a generation that can:

- Recite the Six Pillars by memory,
- Quote Arabic terms,
- Parrot scholarly names…

…but still walk away **spiritually unmoved**.

Why?

Because we're teaching īmān like a checklist. Like data. Like trivia.

We teach creed like it's something to **understand**, not something to **bleed for**.

But the Companions didn't cry under PowerPoints.

They wept under verses.

They changed under truth that **seared their hearts**, not padded their notes.

You cannot ice a soul into awakening.

You must set it on fire.

Faith Must Be Caught, Not Just Taught

The Prophet ﷺ didn't say, "Here's a curriculum."

He **lit people up**.

His words shook sinners.

His face radiated certainty.

His silence spoke louder than speeches.

When he talked about Allah, it felt like the **sky was cracking open**.

When he warned about Hell, hearts trembled.

When he promised Jannah, grown men sobbed.

Because his da'wah wasn't cold.

It was **fire and mercy, thunder and tenderness** — all at once.

"Give glad tidings and do not repel. Make it easy and do not make it hard."

—Prophet Muhammad ﷺ

We're Losing Souls To Boredom, Not Just Doubt

Today, youth leave Islam not just from ideology — but **from indifference**.

Not because someone convinced them Islam is false, but because no one ever showed them Islam is *alive*.

We hand them creed like a dry textbook and expect them to feel awe.

We answer doubts with definitions, not **burning conviction**.

We teach God's names like a vocabulary list — instead of like a call to tremble, trust, and transform.

The truth is:

If our teaching is cold, their hearts will stay frozen.

We Need To Stop Sounding Safe

Faith is not safe.

It demands everything from you: your ego, your desires, your sleep, your plans.

We must stop presenting Islam like it's a **mild lifestyle suggestion**.

It's not a culture.

It's not a trend.

It's **a divine interruption**. A rupture. A **command**.

"Say: My prayer, my sacrifice, my life, and my death are for Allah."

—Surah al-Anʿām (6:162)

When we teach creed, we must sound like we believe it will **save or damn a soul**.

Because it will.

What Preaching With Fire Looks Like

You don't need to scream.

You don't need to be dramatic.

But your **belief must radiate** from your voice, your body, your eyes.

Preaching with fire means:

- **Talking about Hell like it's real.**
- **Mentioning Allah's names with awe.**
- **Speaking of the Prophet ﷺ like he's your hero, not a footnote.**
- **Telling young Muslims that conviction is worth dying for.**
- **Using real life — not just theory — to show faith in action.**

It means being **unapologetically passionate**.

Because passion moves people. Ice does not.

To Teachers, Parents, Khateebs, And Du'āt

Your job is not to inform. It's to **ignite**.

You are not just passing on knowledge.

You are shaping destinies.

- Your classroom might be the only place a kid hears Allah's name said with love.
- Your khutbah might be the spark that keeps someone from leaving Islam.
- Your dinner conversation might be the only dawah your child ever really feels.

This isn't a side job.

This is the frontline.

And if you are cold, dry, bored, or apologetic — you are not neutral. You are in the way.

Faith Must Hit The Heart Before It Hits The Mind

Don't answer every question with a citation.

Start with a story. A feeling. A moment. A tear.

The mind justifies.

But the **heart decides**.

We have minds filled with data but hearts untouched by fire.

Because we keep aiming for the head before lighting the soul.

You must preach like **you've seen the fire**. Like **Jannah is behind your eyes**. Like **this creed is the air you breathe**.

Clarity Challenge: Turn The Flame Back On

Ask yourself:

"When was the last time I spoke about Allah and couldn't stop because I *felt it*?"

"Would I want my child or student to catch *my* version of belief?"

Then take one core truth — maybe a name of Allah, maybe a verse — and **teach it like your life depends on it**.

Not polished. Not perfect.

But real. Fierce. Honest. On fire.

That's how the next generation will believe.

PART III: THE TORCHBEARERS

Creating the Ideological Generation

You've reclaimed the creed.

You've rebuilt your clarity.

Now comes the question that decides everything:

Will you carry it forward—or let it fade again?

In a world tearing down truth and reshaping fitrah, it's no longer enough to survive.

We must raise a generation that can **stand, speak, and lead** with conviction.

This section is your field manual for building the next wave of ideological believers — the ones who won't fold under pressure or apologize for divine guidance.

You'll walk through:

How to make belief a shield in the age of moral collapse

How to guard the heart from doubt *before* it invades

How to raise children who carry creed like a sword, not a slogan

How to prepare for the **Great Test** — when standing for truth will cost everything

This isn't just about holding the flame.

It's about **passing it on — brighter, fiercer, and unshaken**.

Because Islam doesn't survive through information.

It survives through **torchbearers**.

CHAPTER 9: THE CREED AS RESISTANCE

"You don't survive the storm by blending in. You survive by standing up."

We Are Living Through An Ideological War

Make no mistake: this is not a time of peace.

It may look calm on the surface—no bombs, no tanks—but under the surface, a war is raging:

- A war on truth.
- A war on divine purpose.
- A war on fitrah, family, morality, and meaning.

And at the center of the attack?

Your **belief**.

Because if they can hijack your creed, they don't need your masjid.

If they can weaken your conviction, they don't need to silence your Qur'an.

You'll censor yourself. You'll retreat quietly. You'll blend in until there's nothing left to resist with.

That's why this chapter exists.

Creed Is Not A Noun. It's A Shield.

When you say *La ilaha illa Allah* with clarity, you are doing more than affirming truth.

You are:

- **Rejecting all false gods**, including self, society, and state.
- **Declaring loyalty to divine command**, even if it costs you friends, comfort, or safety.
- **Taking a stand** in a world that keeps telling you to sit down.

This is why the early Muslims were **persecuted for belief**.

Not because they were violent. But because they were **clear**.

Because belief, when lived fully, is always seen as a **threat to falsehood**.

The World Is Pressuring You To Be Soft

You are told:

- "Keep your beliefs private."
- "Don't judge others."
- "Islam is fine—as long as it doesn't challenge modern values."

Translation?

"You can believe in Allah—as long as you obey our rules."

That's not tolerance.

That's **ideological occupation**.

If you must hide your faith to keep peace, then your faith is **not at peace**.

True Belief Is An Act Of Defiance

To believe in Allah's authority in a world obsessed with personal freedom?

Defiance.

To declare truth immutable while the world makes everything relative?

Defiance.

To wear your deen unapologetically—hijab, beard, salah, identity—in public?

Defiance.

To say "No" when the world pressures you to say "Maybe"?

Resistance.

And here's the paradox: the more confidently you believe, the more *free* you become.

Because submission to Allah is the **only path to resisting everything else**.

Conviction Is Stronger Than Popularity

Everyone is selling you survival tactics:

- "Stay quiet."
- "Keep a low profile."
- "Adapt your religion for modern life."
- "Don't be too strict—it turns people off."

But history belongs to those who **stood firm**, not those who *fit in*.

- Bilāl wasn't popular. He was loud.
- Ibn Taymiyyah wasn't diplomatic. He was bold.
- Imām Aḥmad didn't compromise. He was **convicted**.

And now we quote them. We name our sons after them.

Because their creed outlived their chains.

The Tools Of Resistance Are Not What You Think

We are not calling for rebellion. We are calling for **resilience**.

Not chaos—but clarity.

Your weapons are:

- **Clarity of belief**: no confusion, no compromise
- **Visible worship**: praying on time, in public, without shame
- **Speaking truth**: even when it's not "palatable"
- **Protecting values**: in your home, school, career, and community
- **Unity with the like-hearted**: because isolated hearts die faster

You don't need a mic to resist.

You need **conviction in your chest and submission on your tongue**.

Don't Let Silence Become Surrender

If you're quiet long enough, you'll forget how to speak.

If you blend in long enough, you'll forget who you are.

There is no neutral ground in a war of beliefs.

Every day, you are either:

- **Preserving the flame**, or
- **Letting it die for the sake of peace that's not really peace.**

Clarity Challenge: Declare Your Resistance

Ask yourself:

"Where have I been blending in to survive instead of standing up to believe?"

Then choose one area—work, school, media, friendships—and take **one visible step** to:

- Pray unapologetically
- Speak the truth gently but firmly
- Dress, act, or live in a way that makes it clear:

"I serve Allah—not culture."

This is how resistance begins: not with protest signs, but with **unshakable loyalty to the creed**.

CHAPTER 10: THE FORTRESS HEART – GUARDING FAITH IN THE AGE OF DOUBT

"It's easier to protect a burning heart than to relight a dead one."

Doubt Isn't A Storm. It's A Slow Leak.

Most Muslims don't lose their faith overnight.

It happens gradually:

- A whisper here.
- A question ignored.
- A TikTok clip that unsettles.
- A meme that mocks.
- A friend who asks, "But *why* do you believe?"

And instead of guarding the heart, we leave it exposed—open tabs, open timelines, open insecurities.

Until one day, the fire is still flickering…

…but the warmth is gone.

Your Heart Is A Fortress—If You Build It

The Prophet ﷺ Told Us:

"In the body there is a piece of flesh: if it is sound, the whole body is sound; if it is corrupt, the whole body is corrupt. It is the heart."

—Sahih al-Bukhari

So the heart must be **guarded like a fortress**.

Not weak and reactive.

Not casually exposed to every passing idea.

But defended. Maintained. Strengthened.

Because once a heart is compromised, no amount of knowledge can make it whole again.

The Entry Points Of Doubt

Doubt creeps in through multiple doors. Here are the most dangerous:

1. **Unfiltered content** – Platforms that mock, distort, or subtly ridicule Islam under the guise of "discussion."
2. **Shallow belief** – Knowing *what* you believe but not *why* or *how* to live it.
3. **Spiritual dryness** – Doubt grows fastest where **dhikr dies** and **Qur'an is absent**.
4. **Ego** – Wanting Islam to bend to your lifestyle instead of bending to Allah's will.
5. **Emotional wounds** – Trauma, grief, or injustice that was never spiritually processed.
6. **Isolation** – A heart with no righteous companionship is a heart under siege.

Doubt Loves A Mind That's Disconnected From The Soul

Some try to solve doubt by throwing more content at it.

More lectures. More books. More YouTube playlists.

But here's the secret:

Most doubts are not intellectual. They're emotional.

The doubt says:

"Islam is hard."

"Why doesn't this make me happy?"

"What if they're right and we're wrong?"

These aren't philosophical puzzles.

They're **cracks in the heart**. And only spiritual clarity can heal them.

How To Build The Fortress

Here's how to reinforce your heart so it doesn't collapse when the next wave hits:

1. Seal the Gates

Limit your exposure to content that:

- Sows confusion
- Glorifies disbelief
- Distorts Islamic values
- Trains your brain to scroll past sacred truth

"Don't argue with people who deny truth for sport." – Ibn Taymiyyah (paraphrased)

It's not cowardice. It's *precaution*.

2. Flood the Heart with Dhikr

Dhikr isn't extra. It's oxygen.

- Say *SubḥānAllah* with reflection.
- Say *Astaghfirullāh* with desperation.
- Say *Allāhu Akbar* until your ego shrinks.
- Read the Qur'an like it's **rescue**, not routine.

A heart that **remembers Allah often** is harder to invade.

3. Convert Questions into Du'ā'

Questions aren't bad—*but don't only Google them.*

Turn them into prayers:

"O Allah, show me the truth as truth and give me the strength to follow it."

"O Allah, protect my heart from lies disguised as insight."

"O Allah, make me love what You love."

Du'ā' keeps your heart **connected to the Source**, not just to screens.

4. Don't Walk Alone

You need people who:

- Speak clarity
- Live with conviction
- Remind you of Jannah
- Call you out when you drift

Isolation is spiritual suicide.

Even the strongest hearts crack without company.

5. Respond with Action, Not Just Answers

When you feel doubt, **don't freeze**.

- Make wudū'.
- Give charity.
- Read Qur'an aloud.
- Call a righteous friend.
- Do **something that asserts belief over hesitation**.

Truth is not only defended with words—it is defended with **obedience**.

Don't Feed The Doubt Monster

Some think: "Maybe I should explore the doubt more. See where it takes me."

But doubts don't leave when entertained. They grow.

The more you feed it, the more it feeds on you.

You don't entertain the thief at the gate. You **lock the door**.

Clarity Challenge: Conduct A Heart Security Audit

Tonight, ask:

"What content am I consuming that weakens my clarity?"

"What habits make it easier for doubt to settle in?"

"Who around me normalizes weak belief?"

Then choose:

- One app to delete
- One habit to build
- One person to reach out to for spiritual companionship

Your heart is your **battlefield**. Guard it like everything depends on it—**because it does**.

CHAPTER 11: RAISING LIONS – INSTILLING CREED IN THE NEXT GENERATION

"Don't raise children who fit in. Raise believers who lead the roar."

They're Not Just Kids. They're The Next Ummah.

We often say, *"The youth are the future."*

No. They're the *present*. And they're under attack.

Every screen, trend, and ideology is fighting for your child's soul.

And if you're not building their īmān, someone else is building their doubt.

You cannot outsource this.

Not to weekend schools.

Not to masjid programs.

Not to your own childhood nostalgia.

Creed is not inherited. It must be instilled—personally, powerfully, and purposefully.

The First Generation Believed Young

Look at the Companions:

- ʿAlī accepted Islam at 10.
- Asmā' bint Abī Bakr risked her life as a teen.
- Musʿab ibn ʿUmair became the first ambassador of Islam before 30.
- Ibn ʿAbbās mastered tafsīr in his early twenties.
- Usāmah ibn Zayd led an army before many today finish college.

Islam didn't wait for them to grow up.

It gave them creed and mission early.

They weren't raised to be safe.

They were raised to be *sent*.

Modern Muslim Youth Are Being Softened By Design

Today, many Muslim kids:

- Know how to take selfies, but not how to take a stand.
- Are fluent in trends, but illiterate in tawḥīd.
- Are praised for good grades but left unequipped for spiritual warfare.
- Are taught to be nice—but never to be *brave*.

We give them gadgets but not guidance.

We protect their comfort but not their convictions.

And then we wonder why they drift.

Belief Must Come Before Identity

We obsess over giving our children a "Muslim identity."

But identity without **ideology** is fragile.

- You can't raise confident Muslims if they don't know *why* they're Muslim.
- You can't expect resistance if they've never tasted *conviction*.
- You can't demand modesty, prayer, or loyalty—if you haven't **lit the fire behind it**.

Raise īmān before you raise expectations.

You Must Preach With Fire At Home

If your child doesn't see you excited about Islam, why should they be?

They need to:

- Hear you speak about Allah with love and awe.
- See you prioritize ṣalāh over everything.
- Watch you repent out loud.
- Know that **your Islam costs you something—and it's worth it**.

You're not just raising a child.

You're modeling surrender.

They will learn far more from your **tone than your rules**.

The Goal Is Not "Good Kids." The Goal Is Lions.

Raise kids who:

- Know the six pillars of īmān **and how they reshape daily life**.
- Understand tawḥīd not as theory—but as **a sword, a shield, and a compass**.

- Can answer, "Why do you believe?" without flinching.
- Know that resisting trends is not weird—it's worship.
- Are **emotionally connected** to the Prophet ﷺ, not just familiar with his name.

You're not raising people-pleasers.

You're raising those who can **say "La ilaha illa Allah" when the world says "follow your truth."**

Build A Creed-Centered Home

This isn't about building a "religious atmosphere."

It's about building an **ideological fortress**.

Try this:

- Make tafsīr part of your family language.
- Play lectures with fire, not fluff.
- Speak of Allah's power often—*really often*.
- Tell stories of the Companions like legends—because they were.
- Involve your kids in your du'ā' so they hear what you beg Allah for.

Let your home say, without words:

"Here, we believe. Here, Allah reigns."

Don't Wait For A Crisis

Most parents begin caring about their child's creed **after a breakdown**:

- "He said he's not sure if Islam is true."
- "She said hijab doesn't make sense anymore."
- "He's dating, and I don't know how to talk to him."

Don't wait for doubt to knock.

Install the armor now.

Belief must be **clear before it's challenged**.

It must be **loved before it's tested**.

It must be **lived before it's debated**.

Clarity Challenge: Build One Daily Creed Habit

Pick one action that connects your children (or students) to īmān every day:

- A story.
- A verse reflection.
- One of Allah's names.
- A 5-minute creed check-in.

Not long. Not complicated.

Just consistent fire.

Enough to keep their hearts warm when the world turns cold.

CHAPTER 12: THE FINAL STAND – PREPARING FOR THE GREAT TEST

"The test isn't coming. It's already here. The only question is: will you stand?"

Every Age Has Its Fitnah. This Is Ours.

The Companions had swords at their necks.

Muslims in Andalus were expelled or forced to convert.

Scholars in every century faced lashes, exile, and death.

Today?

We face a different sword: one of ideology, identity, and slow, silent surrender.

- You're told to **hide your beliefs** in the name of tolerance.
- You're told to **adapt the dīn** for progress.
- You're told to **never judge**, even when truth is mocked.
- You're told to **apologize for believing clearly**.

This is not neutrality. This is the final test.

The War Is For Your Mind

The battlefield is no longer just in media or politics.

It's in:

- The school classroom
- The Netflix algorithm
- The HR department
- The university syllabus
- The YouTube short
- The influencer's story
- Your own internal monologue

The world doesn't ask you to leave Islam.

It asks you to **mold it**.

To **reinterpret it**.

To say, *"I'm Muslim, but…"*

That's not faith.

That's **preparing to fold**.

Truth Will Become Strange Again

The Prophet ﷺ told us:

"Islam began as something strange and will return to being strange. So glad tidings to the strangers."

—Sahih Muslim

We are entering that era.

Being principled will look "extreme."

Being modest will look "oppressive."

Being loyal to revelation will look "backwards."

But the Prophet ﷺ didn't say, "Avoid being strange."

He said, **rejoice** — because those who remain loyal in that time are the true torchbearers.

The Great Test Will Cost Something

Make no mistake: it won't be easy.

You may lose:

- Opportunities
- Jobs
- Friendships
- Approval
- Even your safety

But if you don't prepare to **lose for your Lord**, you've already surrendered.

This dīn wasn't built on convenience.

It was built on **sacrifice**, **clarity**, and **eternal reward**.

The Signs Are Already Here

We are not speculating. The signs of collapse are visible:

- Muslim children who can't explain their faith.
- Adults ashamed of verses that offend modern ears.
- Influencers who say "Islam is personal" as they twist it for views.
- Families falling apart under liberal redefinitions of love and freedom.
- Masjids too afraid to speak clearly.
- An ummah with access to revelation but allergic to submission.

This is the calm before the storm.

And this book?

It's your war manual.

Who Will Be The Final Line?

You've rebuilt your creed.

You've fortified your heart.

You've begun raising the next generation.

But now comes the question:

"Will you stand firm when the world shakes?"

"Will you protect the flame when it's easier to let it go?"

"Will you say *La ilaha illa Allah* when it costs you something?"

Because the final test won't just measure what you know.

It will measure what you **won't compromise**.

Hat Standing Looks Like

This is not about bravado or recklessness.

This is about **quiet, unshakable loyalty** when others bow to pressure.

To stand in the Great Test means:

- You guard your family even when the culture mocks you.
- You speak the truth even when you lose followers.
- You live the creed even when it isolates you.
- You say "no" when the entire room says "yes."
- You die on this dīn, not just live on it.

"Among the believers are men who were true to what they pledged to Allah…"

—Surah al-Aḥzāb (33:23)

Be one of them.

Clarity Challenge: Write Your Pledge

Tonight, write a personal creed pledge. No one needs to see it.

Start with:

"I will stand by the truth of Islam even if…"

Then fill in the blanks:

- …I lose friendships
- …I face slander
- …I am misunderstood
- …I feel fear

Read it. Mean it.

Let your soul **sign it with sincerity**.

Because the test is coming.

The time to prepare is *now*.

CLOSING MANIFESTO: THE 10 COMMANDMENTS OF CLARITY

"In an age of confusion, clarity is an act of worship—and a form of resistance."

1. Submit First, Ask Second

Faith begins with surrender.

You don't need every answer to obey.

Obedience opens the heart; questions refine it later.

"We hear and we obey." — That's clarity.

2. Treat Tawḥīd As The Center Of Everything

Not a chapter. Not a topic. Not a theory.

Tawḥīd is the lens. The starting point. The end goal.

Raise children on it. Judge culture by it.

Speak it, teach it, and live it like it **owns you**.

3. Guard The Heart Like A Fortress

Doubt enters when the heart is unguarded.

Control your inputs. Limit ideological noise. Flood your soul with dhikr.

Don't just protect your mind—protect your **devotion**.

4. Build Creed Into Habits, Not Just Thoughts

Faith isn't what you say in a halaqah—it's how you act under pressure.

Build daily habits that embed belief into muscle memory:

- Salah first.
- Du'ā' often.
- Qur'an daily.
- Gratitude loudly.
- Tawakkul practically.

5. Speak Clearly—Even When It's Unpopular

Stop softening Islam to make it more "palatable."

Truth is a mercy when spoken with conviction.

Be the one who says what others are too afraid to.

You are not here to blend in. You are here to speak for Allah.

6. Teach Creed Like It's Life And Death

Because it is.

Don't make belief sound boring.

Preach with **fire, urgency, and love**.

Let your family and students feel that **you believe this with every fiber of your being**.

7. Build An Ummah Of Torchbearers

Find your people. Build your circle.

Surround yourself with those who:

- Believe fiercely
- Obey visibly
- Protect creed collectively
- Clarity doesn't survive in isolation. It multiplies in community.

8. Reject Confusion As Normal

Just because the world is lost doesn't mean you have to be.

Confusion is not humility. Doubt is not sophistication.

Allah didn't send a foggy book. He sent **light**.

Don't glorify gray when you were made for guidance.

9. Expect The Test—And Prepare For It

Clarity will cost you.

Be ready to lose comfort, clout, or company for Allah's sake.

The storm is coming. Get your shield on.

Those who stand firm when truth is unpopular are the ones who inherit it forever.

10. Say La Ilaha Illa Allah With Your Life

Not just your lips.

Say it with your time.

Say it with your money.

Say it with your parenting, your silence, your speech, your resistance.

This one sentence is your sword, your shield, and your salvation.

⬜ Bonus: Clarity Rituals – Your Daily Practice

1. **Morning:** Read a verse of Qur'an and apply it to your day.
2. **Afternoon:** Make du'ā' for clarity and courage.
3. **Evening:** Audit your actions: *Did I live what I believe today?*
4. **Weekly:** Teach one truth to someone—your child, friend, or follower.
5. **Monthly:** Review your creed. Reinforce it. Realign your loyalty.

Your Final Role

You are not just a reader.

You are now a **torchbearer of clarity**.

In a world of blurry beliefs and shaky faith, your clarity is da'wah.

Your courage is mercy.

Your firmness is light.

Say it.

Live it.

Die on it.

La ilaha illa Allah.

CONCLUSION

"Clarity was never the end goal. Conviction is."

S o now you know.

You know how we lost clarity — slowly, subtly, tragically.

You know where it was buried — under complexity, fear, and borrowed philosophies.

You know how to find it again — in the Qur'an, the Prophet's example, and the lived fire of the early generations.

But this book was never meant to be an intellectual exercise.

It was meant to be a **catalyst**.

You didn't just read about creed.

You rebuilt it.

You didn't just learn the Six Pillars.

You stood them back up in your soul.

You didn't just think about doubt.

You fortified your heart against it.

You didn't just study clarity.

You became a torchbearer of it.

This Is Not The End — It's The Assignment

What you've gained here is not a conclusion.

It's a **commission**.

A commission to:

- Speak clearly when others stay vague
- Stand firm when others bend
- Teach children who won't just "be Muslim" — but *live Islam*
- Preach with fire, not ice
- Love the truth more than your reputation
- Live *La ilaha illa Allah* — in traffic, in meetings, in fear, in joy, in loss, in the public square, and behind closed doors

You are not just a reader now.

You are a carrier of creed.

A witness to the truth.

A builder of the ideological generation.

One Final Reminder

There is a storm.

But there is also a flame.

You've seen it. You've touched it.

Now you must **guard it. Feed it. And pass it on.**

The world doesn't need more information.

It needs **conviction**.

It needs **you**.

Say it.

Live it.

ABDELLATIF RAJI

Die on it.

And pass it forward.

La ilaha illa Allah.

EPILOGUE

"It was never just something to say. It was something to live. To love. To die for."

La ilaha illa Allah

There is no deity worthy of worship but Allah.

Seven words.

Four in Arabic.

One flame.

This sentence split history.

It made tyrants tremble and slaves rise.

It turned shepherds into scholars, rebels into leaders, and orphans into men who shook empires.

It is not just the foundation of Islam.

It is the **foundation of sanity**, the **correction of every lie**, the **end of every false god**.

It demands your love.

It demands your loyalty.

It demands your life.

Not once.

But **every single day.**

Say It Like It's Oxygen

Say it when you're doubting.

Say it when you're ashamed.

Say it when you're afraid.

Say it when you feel nothing at all.

Say it until your soul remembers who owns it.

Say: **La ilaha illa Allah.**

Let it rewire your instincts.

Let it purify your desires.

Let it burn down every idol you've built in your heart.

Let it lift your face when the world pulls it down.

Let it be the first thing on your lips when you wake,

and the last thing when you return to Him.

One Sentence. One Life.

You don't need more information.

You need more submission.

You need more remembrance.

You need more **clarity in the fog**.

And it begins here:

Not with a new idea.

Not with a new movement.

But with the oldest truth, spoken clearly, lived fully:

La ilaha illa Allah.

Don't just say it.

Become it.

AFTERWORD

If you've made it to this point, I want to thank you.

Not for reading the book — but for *fighting through the fog with me.*

You've walked through broken mirrors, reclaimed the pure spring, and stood among torchbearers.

You've wrestled with big questions and sat with uncomfortable truths.

You've faced a forgotten creed and helped bring it back into focus.

This was never just a book.

It was always a **battlefield**.

And you made it through — page by page, truth by truth, challenge by challenge.

What Comes Next

Now comes the hard part: **living it**.

- Living with clarity when culture calls for compromise
- Speaking with conviction when silence is easier
- Teaching your children creed that costs something
- Being a source of guidance in a world of noise

You don't need to be perfect. You just need to be **clear**, **loyal**, and **lit**

from within.

From Here On, You're Not Just A Reader

You're a **torchbearer**.

Someone who carries īmān not as theory, but as *truth with teeth* — something that shapes homes, communities, decisions, and legacies.

Wherever you go from here — may the flame stay alive.

If this book stirred you, share it.

If it challenged you, sit with it again.

If it gave you clarity — then become someone else's clarity.

And if one day your children, your students, or your people ask,

"How do I know what's true?"

You'll have an answer.

A clear one.

The only one that ever really mattered:

La ilaha illa Allah.

APPENDIX: 100 QUESTIONS YOU DON'T NEED TO ANSWER TO BELIEVE

"Surrender isn't stupidity. It's clarity."

Introduction

We are drowning in questions.

Some sincere.

Some weaponized.

Some designed to delay submission.

Some designed to erode it.

But here's a truth most people will never tell you:

You don't need to answer every question to believe.

The desert Bedouin didn't need philosophical proofs.

The Sahabah didn't wait for full understanding before saying yes.

The early Muslims didn't freeze when challenged.

They heard. They believed. They moved.

This appendix is your reminder: **You are allowed to believe without needing to out-debate the internet.**

Here are 100 questions — real, imagined, hypothetical, and sometimes ridiculous — that **you don't need to answer** before you submit to *La ilaha illa Allah.*

If they matter, you'll learn in time.

If they don't, you'll be grateful you didn't waste your īmān chasing smoke.

How To Use This Appendix

- **Permission to stop chasing every doubt**
- **A reminder to re-center submission over speculation**
- **A tool for educators, parents, and du'āt** to answer doubt with perspective, not panic
- **A lifeline for Muslims overwhelmed by modern discourse**

Existence Of God & Philosophy

1. Can God's existence be proven through logic alone?
2. If everything needs a cause, who created God?
3. If God is infinite, how can we know anything about Him?
4. Why is belief necessary if reason can't fully grasp God?
5. Isn't belief without empirical evidence irrational?
6. Can science disprove the supernatural?
7. What if the universe just exists without a creator?
8. If God is perfect, why does He "want" worship?
9. Can God create a rock so heavy He can't lift it?
10. What if we're just brains in a simulation?

Divine Will, Justice & Suffering

1. Why does God allow innocent people to suffer?
2. Why create people destined for Hell?
3. If God knows the future, do we really have free will?
4. How is it just to punish eternally for finite sins?
5. Why are some people born into suffering while others live in ease?
6. Isn't predestination fatalistic?
7. Why do bad people seem to thrive while believers struggle?
8. What's the point of du'ā' if Allah already knows the outcome?
9. Why does Allah test believers more than others?
10. Why do natural disasters kill people who did nothing wrong?

Prophethood & Revelation

1. Why didn't God send multiple prophets to every generation?
2. Why didn't the Prophet ﷺ perform more miracles on demand?
3. Why wasn't the Qur'an revealed all at once?
4. What if the Qur'an is just Muhammad's words?
5. Why didn't the Prophet ﷺ live in our time?
6. Why should I trust the hadith literature?
7. What if the Companions made mistakes in transmission?
8. Could the Qur'an have been edited over time?
9. Isn't it possible that Islam borrowed ideas from other religions?
10. Why do other scriptures also claim to be from God?

Sharia, Law & Ethics

1. Why are there punishments like stoning or hand-cutting?
2. Isn't Islamic law outdated in modern society?
3. Why are there gender differences in inheritance and testimony?
4. Why is homosexuality forbidden if people are born that way?
5. Why are apostasy and blasphemy punishable in classical law?
6. Why does Islam regulate clothing, food, and finance?
7. Why can't Muslims marry outside the religion freely?
8. Why is music or dancing controversial?
9. What's the wisdom behind ritual slaughter or hijab?
10. Isn't Sharia oppressive to women?

Sectarianism, History & Politics

1. Why are there so many sects in Islam?
2. Who's right — Sunnis, Shi'a, Sufis, Salafis?
3. What about the violence in Islamic history?
4. Why did the early Muslims fight each other?
5. What if some of the Companions were wrong or corrupt?
6. How do I trust scholars when so many disagree?
7. Isn't the concept of a Caliphate outdated?
8. What's the point of Islamic governance in a secular world?
9. Can't Islam evolve politically with time?
10. Shouldn't religion be separate from politics?

Contemporary Culture & Identity

1. Isn't it intolerant to say Islam is the only true path?

2. What if a good non-Muslim is better than a sinful Muslim?
3. Can't I just be spiritual without following religion?
4. Isn't religion a man-made concept used to control people?
5. What if all religions lead to the same God?
6. Isn't morality subjective?
7. How can I balance modern values and Islamic ethics?
8. Why does Islam restrict sexual freedom or personal expression?
9. What about gender identity and transgender issues in Islam?
10. Can Muslims be fully modern and fully religious?

Psychological, Emotional & Personal Doubts

1. Why don't I feel anything in prayer?
2. What if I'm just Muslim because of my parents?
3. Why do I feel numb when reading Qur'an?
4. What if I die with weak faith?
5. What if Allah doesn't forgive me?
6. Why do I struggle to love Allah or fear Hell?
7. Am I a hypocrite if I have doubts?
8. What if I lose my faith one day?
9. Why do I sometimes wish Islam were easier?
10. Why is staying consistent so hard?

Science, Evolution & Modern Thought

1. What if evolution disproves the story of Adam?
2. How can religion be true if science keeps changing?
3. What about ancient cosmology in the Qur'an?
4. Did humans really descend from a single pair?

5. How do we reconcile miracles with natural law?
6. What about Qur'anic verses that don't match modern science?
7. Can a rational person believe in jinn or angels?
8. Isn't religion anti-science?
9. What if the mind is just neurons and chemistry?
10. Why do some scholars reject modern psychology?

Media Narratives & Public Perception

1. Isn't Islam inherently violent?
2. What about terrorism committed in the name of Islam?
3. Why does the media portray Muslims so negatively?
4. Why are Islamic leaders silent on global injustice?
5. Why do some Muslims say one thing and do another?
6. Why do Muslim countries violate human rights?
7. Can I still be proud to be Muslim in a post-9/11 world?
8. Why does the West hate Islam?
9. Isn't Islam a threat to modern democracy?
10. Why do Muslims seem so defensive all the time?

Pop Culture, Satire & Ridicule

1. What if Islam is just a meme — like all religions?
2. What if the flying donkey is just mythology?
3. What about TikTok "ex-Muslims" who seem convincing?
4. How can I believe when religion is mocked everywhere?
5. What if religious devotion is just psychological conditioning?
6. Why does religion feel "cringe" in modern spaces?
7. What if faith is just fear of death dressed up?
8. What if AI and science replace the need for God?

9. What if the Qur'an is just ancient poetry?

10. What if we're wrong — and nobody knows the truth?

The Answer You Need

You do not need to answer all these to stand on truth.

Faith is not about silencing every critic.

It's about **recognizing the clarity Allah already gave you** — and surrendering to it.

La ilaha illa Allah is not proven by solving every doubt.

It is proven by living it — with trust, devotion, and clarity.

Final Word

Some questions are worth deep study.

Some are worth putting on a shelf.

Some are worth ignoring altogether.

But **none of them** cancel out this truth:

La ilaha illa Allah.

It is clear.

It is complete.

And it is enough.

ABOUT THE AUTHOR

The author is not a scholar by title — but a student by necessity.

A lifelong autodidact, he came to the study of creed not through academic institutions or formal certifications, but through an urgent hunger for truth in an age drowning in confusion.

Frustrated by the fog of over-intellectualized discourse, spiritual performance, and inherited jargon, he began a personal project to return to the source:

the Book, the Prophet ﷺ, and the way of the earliest believers.

What began as a personal journey turned into a mission:

To help others **reclaim clarity, live creed**, and **raise a generation unshaken by modern confusion**.

He writes not as a preacher, but as a peer.

Not to impress — but to ignite.

Not to build followers — but to awaken **torchbearers**.

This book is the fruit of that mission.

And it is only the beginning.

For inquiries, speaking engagements, or consulting, reach out via:

https://www.yaraak.com